Photo by Susan Johann © 1998

The set from the Signature Theatre Company production of *Mr. Peters' Connections*. Set design by Francis O'Connor.

MR. PETERS' CONNECTIONS

BY ARTHUR MILLER

★

DRAMATISTS
PLAY SERVICE
INC.

MR. PETERS' CONNECTIONS
Copyright © 1999, Arthur Miller
ALL RIGHTS RESERVED

CAUTION: Professionals and amateurs are hereby warned that performance of MR. PETERS' CONNECTIONS is subject to a royalty. It is fully protected under the copyright laws of the United States of America, and of all countries covered by the International Copyright Union (including the Dominion of Canada and the rest of the British Commonwealth), and of all countries covered by the Pan-American Copyright Convention, the Universal Copyright Convention, the Berne Convention, and of all countries with which the United States has reciprocal copyright relations. All rights, including professional/amateur stage rights, motion picture, recitation, lecturing, public reading, radio broadcasting, television, video or sound recording, all other forms of mechanical or electronic reproduction, such as CD-ROM, CD-I, DVD, information storage and retrieval systems and photocopying, and the rights of translation into foreign languages, are strictly reserved. Particular emphasis is placed upon the matter of readings, permission for which must be secured from the Author's agent in writing.

The stage performance rights in MR. PETERS' CONNECTIONS (other than first class rights) are controlled exclusively by the DRAMATISTS PLAY SERVICE, INC., 440 Park Avenue South, New York, N.Y. 10016. No professional or non-professional performance of the Play (excluding first class professional performance) may be given without obtaining in advance the written permission of the DRAMATISTS PLAY SERVICE, INC., and paying the requisite fee.

Inquiries concerning all other rights should be addressed to International Creative Management, Inc., 40 West 57th Street, New York, N.Y. 10019, Attn: Bridget Aschenberg.

SPECIAL NOTE

Anyone receiving permission to produce MR. PETERS' CONNECTIONS is required (1) to give credit to the Author as sole and exclusive Author of the Play on the title page of all programs distributed in connection with performances of the Play and in all instances in which the title of the Play appears for purposes of advertising, publicizing or otherwise exploiting the Play and/or a production thereof. The name of the Author must appear on a separate line, in which no other name appears, immediately beneath the title and in size of type equal to 50% of the largest, most prominent letter used for the title of the Play. No person, firm or entity may receive credit larger or more prominent than that accorded the Author; and (2) to give the following acknowledgment on the title page of all programs distributed in connection with performances of the Play:

World premiere production produced by Signature Theatre Company, New York City.
James Houghton, Founding Artistic Director
Thomas C. Proehl, Managing Director
Elliot Fox, Associate Director

SPECIAL NOTE ON SONGS AND RECORDINGS

For performance of the songs, arrangements and recordings mentioned in this Play that are protected by copyright, the permission of the copyright owners must be obtained; or other songs, arrangements and recordings in the public domain substituted.

Preface for
MR. PETERS' CONNECTIONS

A play ought to explain — or not explain — itself, but a play with both living and dead characters interacting may justifiably ask for a word or two of explanation.

Mr. Peters is in that suspended state of consciousness which can come upon a man taking a nap, when the mind, still close to consciousness and self-awareness, is freed to roam from real memories to conjectures, from trivialities to tragic insights, from terror of death to glorying in one's being alive. The play, in short, is taking place inside Mr. Peters' mind, or at least on its threshold from where it is still possible to glance back toward daylight life or forward into the misty depths.

Mr. Peters is, of course, alive. So is his wife, as well as Rose, who turns out to be their daughter, and Leonard, her boyfriend. Adele, the black bag lady is neither dead or alive, but simply Peters' construct, the to-him incomprehensible black presence on the dim borders of his city life.

Cathy-May is long dead, but the dead in memory do not quite die and often live more vividly than in life. Cathy-May's husband is Peters' conjecture as to what kind of man she might have married, given her nature as he knew it when they were lovers. And Calvin a.k.a. Charley, who turns out to be his brother, is also long dead even if the competition between them is very much alive in Peters' mind along with its fraternal absurdities.

As for the set; it should look like whatever the reader or producer imagines as a space where the living and the dead may meet, the gray or blue or blazing red terrain of the sleeping mind where imagination runs free. Fragments of jazz and sheer-sound should also rise and fall. The stage may be ablaze with light at times or steeped in cavernous darkness at others. It may threaten or reassure, for the action of the play is the procession of Mr. Peters' moods, each of them summoning up the next, all of them strung upon the line of his anxiety, his fear, if you will, that he has not found the secret, the pulsing center of energy — what he calls the subject — that will make his life cohere.

Arthur Miller
December, 1998

MR. PETERS' CONNECTIONS received its world premiere at Signature Theatre Company (James Houghton, Founding Artistic Director; Thomas C. Proehl, Managing Director; Elliot Fox, Associate Director) in New York City, on April 28, 1998. It was directed by Garry Hynes; the set design was by Francis O'Connor; the costume design was by Teresa Snider-Stein; the lighting design was by Beverly Emmons; the sound design was by Red Ramona; and the production stage manager was Amanda W. Sloan. The cast was as follows:

CALVIN	Jeff Weiss
HARRY PETERS	Peter Falk
ADELE	Erica Bradshaw
CATHY-MAE	Kris Carr
LARRY	Daniel Oreskes
LEONARD	Alan Mozes
ROSE	Tari Signor
CHARLOTTE	Anne Jackson

CHARACTERS

CALVIN — Mr. Peters' dead brother.

HARRY PETERS — Retired airline and military pilot and lecturer.

ADELE — A black bag lady.

CATHY-MAE — Mr. Peters' dead lover.

LARRY — Her husband as Peters imagines him.

LEONARD — A guitarist and lover of:

ROSE — Mr. Peters' daughter.

CHARLOTTE — Mr. Peters' wife

MR. PETERS' CONNECTIONS

A broken structure indicating an old, abandoned nightclub in New York City.

A small, dusty upright piano, some chairs, a couple of tables, a few upended.

Three chairs set close to piano with instruments propped up on them — a bass, trumpet, saxophone.

Seated on the banquette, Adele, a black bag lady, is ensconced amid her bags; she is reading Vogue *magazine and sipping from a bottle of wine. She occasionally examines her face in a hand mirror.*

Calvin enters. Peters enters, looking around. Halts.

CALVIN. Well, here it is. *(Silence. Peters very slowly looks at everything. Then goes still.)*
PETERS. *(Undirected to anyone.)* To be moved. Yes. Even once more to feel that thunder, yes. Just once! *(Slight pause.)* Lust aside, what could hit me? Novels? Model airplanes, movies, cooking, the garden? *(Shakes his head, dry grief.)* And yet, deep down ... deep down I always seem on the verge of weeping. God knows why, when I have everything. *(Slight pause; he peers ahead.)* What is the subject? *(Peters goes to the piano, plays the first five notes of "September Song,"* then walks a few steps. The piano continues playing; both men stare into space; piano subsides into silence. Now Calvin gestures toward the structure.)*
CALVIN. Needs some work, of course.

---

*See Special Note on Songs and Recordings on copyright page.

PETERS. My wife should be here in a few minutes, I believe.
CALVIN. She'll like it, most women do.
PETERS. I'm very tired. I've been walking. Why women?
CALVIN. Hard to say. The powder room, maybe.
ADELE. *(Not looking away from her mirror.)* Gorgeous. *(Neither man seems to hear her.)*
PETERS. I take it you're not from here?
CALVIN. You have a good ear. Russia, I guess.
PETERS. You guess!
CALVIN. Who can be sure? In my mother's bed, I suppose, same as everybody else.
PETERS. Mother's bed.
CALVIN. Where I'm from. Actually, Sheepshead Bay, Brooklyn.
PETERS. Actually. But people from Sheepshead Bay, Brooklyn do not say "actually," it's too ... I don't know, high-class. But it doesn't matter; if you'd told me in the first place I'd have forgotten it by now. My personal situation these days is trying to paddle a canoe with a tennis racket ... I am thinking, who does he remind me of?
CALVIN. I tend to do that. Some people, all they do in life is remind people of somebody. — Generally I remind people of somebody nice and reliable.
PETERS. Why don't we leave it right there.
CALVIN. I'm not trying to be facetious ...
PETERS. Listen. Let's settle this — conflict is not my game anymore; or suspense; I really don't like trying to figure out what's going on. Peace and quiet, avoid the bumps, I'm perfectly content just to raise the shade and greet my morning. Not that I'm depressed; in fact, I feel I am an inch away from the most thrilling glass of water I ever had. On that order. *(Cathy-May is lit.)* Oh my. *(Going toward her; sad amazement.)* My-my-my. The flat broad belly, the spring of thighs, how the fire flares up just before it dies...! *(He recognizes her, gasps.)* Good god, Cathy-May! *(Mystified.)* — Then you're not ... you're not ... dead? *(Turns from her.)* How can we go on seeing them if they...? Or ... say now, can she not have-d...? *(Breaks off, thinks.)* But of course she did! *(Freshly affected.)* Of course she did! *(Nearly weeping.)* Of course she did! It snowed on her funeral ... *(Peers for a*

clue, then glances at her.) But where is she, then? *(Barely smiling, shakes his head, mystified, excited.)* — Why am I so happy? *(A tinkling of Mozart* is heard. Cathy-May comes to him; she is naked, in high heels; a big smile breaks onto his face as she approaches. She is giggling.)* Ah yes, how proud of your body — like a new party gown. *(Giggling, with finely honed mock-solemnity she does a formal curtsy with thumbs and forefingers pressed together as though lifting a wide skirt. Laughing softly he bows formally, with one foot thrust forward. They are like two mating birds. Laughing.)* You can't do this kind of dancing dressed like that, darling! *(Still curtsying, she retreats into darkness. Music dies. His laughter sours.)* Or am I depressed?

CALVIN. You've been around.

PETERS. And around again, yes — Pan Am captain twenty-six years. I'm really much older than I look. If you planted an apple tree when I was born you'd be cutting it down for firewood by now.

CALVIN. I was going to say, you don't look all that old.

PETERS. *(A chuckle.)* I am older than everyone I ever knew. All my dogs are dead. Half a dozen cats, parakeets ... all gone. Every pilot I ever flew with. Probably every woman I ever slept with, too, except my wife. I doubt there's a government in the world that hasn't been overthrown at least once since I was born, except for us and England. I still pick up the phone to call some old friend, until I realize ... *(Chuckles.)* ... — Maybe some broken nerve in my brain won't register the vacant pillows and the empty chairs. I wonder sometimes, have I without knowing it been embalmed? Or maybe death is polite, and we must open the door to let him in or he'll just hang around out there on the porch. *(Frowns, mystified.)* — Why am I so fluent? I'm not, usually. I'm known for not saying anything for eight hours at a time. — What about this powder room, why are women so crazy about it? ... I'm enjoying this, but what is the subject?

CALVIN. Women love to redecorate.

PETERS. Oh, of course, yes. A man will never notice the paint

---

*See Special Note on Songs and Recordings on copyright page.

floating off the ceiling onto his head, but a woman can count dust. — You always have an answer, don't you.
CALVIN. Not always.
PETERS. Often, though.
CALVIN. Pretty often.
PETERS. Do you enjoy being so right?
CALVIN. *(Shrugs.)* I can live with it.
PETERS. I'm very different; I enjoy being right but you have to let the woman think they're right so you can take your nap in peace. The older you get, you know, the more you tend to chuckle. I do a lot of it. I mean, who can hit a man when he's chuckling, right? I had a dream, many years ago; this enormous fireplace; and I got up from my chair and said good-bye to my wife, and walked into it. The back of it swung open and I stepped out into the most perfect room I'd ever seen. Everything in that room — the furniture, the color of the walls, the carpet ... it was all absolutely right. Not a single thing out of place or painful to me. And I looked out the window and the street was perfect. And I felt perfect too. It was all so satisfying, as though that is where I really belong. In fact, I begin to yearn for that house every now and then until I realize — and with some surprise, that it never existed. And the subject, you said, was...? Well, never mind. *(Looks about.)* ... I can't imagine anyone thinking he belonged in this place, can you? You absolutely remind me of someone, don't you.
CALVIN. Show your wife the powder room, she'll love you for it.
PETERS. Let's not go into it any further, okay? I have no interest whatsoever in this place. It's not my kind of place at all.
CALVIN. Maybe give it a little time, you might get used to it.
PETERS. *(Chuckles angrily.)* I don't want to get used to it, will you stop irritating me? The only reason I'm even in this neighborhood is ... I can't recall ... oh yes, *(Calvin is motionless, unaffected.)* I decided to buy shoes. I have very narrow feet.
CALVIN. Not as narrow as mine, betcha — triple-A.
PETERS. Quadruple-A. *(Extending a foot.)* Narrow as herrings. — So I said I'd meet her here.
CALVIN. I used to take a quintuple-A but I don't have time

to go running all over the city looking for them anymore ... I am busy!
PETERS.   Well I'm busy too ...
CALVIN.   Nót as busy as I am.
PETERS.   I assure you, I am just as busy as you are. I got these in that shoe store right on the corner.
CALVIN.   You went in *there?*
PETERS.   *(Shamed.)* ... Well only for a couple of minutes.
CALVIN.   Phew! Well, it's your funeral.
PETERS.   *(Embarrassed.)* Why? — what's wrong with going in there?
CALVIN.   There isn't time now; I really need to know what you think of this place? Yes?
PETERS.   Well let's see ... Oh, the hell with this, I'm leaving. *(Starts to go.)*
CALVIN.   You can't!
PETERS.   Don't you tell me I can't, I have very low cholesterol! *(He turns and starts out.)*
CALVIN.   What about your wife?
PETERS.   God, I almost forgot. *(Sits meekly.)* Thanks for reminding me ... You always need a reason to stay. I have to stay because of my wife. Why because of my wife?
CALVIN.   You're meeting her here.
PETERS.   Right, yes! *(Short pause.)* Why am I meeting her here?
CALVIN.   Probably because that was the arrangement.
PETERS.   But why here?
CALVIN.   What's the difference? One has to meet somewhere. *(Cathy-May appears in a filmy dress; Peters goes to her, hesitantly.)*
PETERS.   Could we walk together, darling? Just side by side? I'm sure you can get out of this if you exercise. Please — concentrate, darling! *(Desperately.)* You must try to move more! Here, let me help! *(He gets in front of her, grasps a thigh and gets her to take a stiff, doll-like step. — Alarm in his voice.)* Relax! You must stop being so stiff. *(Angered.)* Why are you doing this, are you spiting me?! Here, do this and stop being an idiot! One-two, one-two ... *(He jumps up and down, flapping his arms. She remains inert. He turns to Calvin.)* Could you applaud? — she loves me, but she's forgotten. *(Calvin claps his hands; she doesn't*

change.) He's applauding, dear ... listen! *(To Calvin, indicating her.)* Are you sure we're both in the same place?
CALVIN.   How can two occupy...?
PETERS.   ... the same space, yes, that's right. *(Moves away from her.)* That's one thing you have to say for the war, you always knew where you had to be ... you had to be where you could get killed, you see. Taking off after a couple of dozen missions you'd naturally wonder, "Is this my last moon?" And so on. But funny, you know? — remarkably little fear — I don't recall actual fear; I suppose because we knew we were good and the Japs were evil, so the whole thing was necessary, and that can soak up fear like a blotter. On that order. *(Desperation, loudly.)* — Whereas now, I just cannot find the subject! Like I'll be strolling down the street, and suddenly I'm weeping, everything welling up — What is the subject? Know what I mean? Simply cannot grasp the subject. — I can't understand why I'm so fluent here!
ADELE.   Something you forgot hasn't forgotten you. You should take up drinking, it might all come pouring out.
PETERS.   But I had a wonderful childhood.
ADELE.   Famous last words.
PETERS.   No-no, in fact, as a kid of sixteen ... good God, I'd bicycle out to Floyd Bennet Field and wash airplanes for the Army pilots. Dollar a plane, plus they taught me to fly those little Stinsons all over the clear Brooklyn sky. Imagine that nowadays, a kid handed the stick of a fighter plane? — things are never going to get that good again, I tell you we had the best of it, the sweetness. Take Pan Am; Pan Am was not an airline, it was a calling, a knighthood. A Pan Am captain ... hell, we were the best of the best and when you took off, the sweaty little corporate statistician, for Christ's sake, did not climb into your lap, they stayed back there on the ground where they belonged. And God — when you got suited up in your whites and your gold epaulettes, the girls inhaled and puffed their feathers and achieved womanhood right in front of your eyes. *(Chuckle.)* I cannot understand why I'm so fluent in this building.
CALVIN.   And what about this place?
PETERS.   I don't flaunt my opinions, but I'd say the best way to redecorate this place would be a small bomb.

CALVIN. Some people think this could be a gold mine.
PETERS. Oh I'm sure! 'Specially the powder room, probably.
CALVIN. Then why do you have this browbeaten attitude?
PETERS. *(Angering.)* Absolutely not! If I were younger I'd be chomping at the bit to get in there ...
CALVIN. But you're skeptical.
PETERS. *(Suddenly in distress.)* I'm asking you to stop talking about this ... you're disturbing me!
CALVIN. Listen, you've got to start facing reality.
PETERS. No-no, I'm too old — facing reality is for the young who still have time to avoid it. An old man talking about a ... a *woman's powder room* — ? — it's obscene! Look at the veins in the back of my hands? — shall these warped fingers stroke a breast, cup an ass...? And you call life fair? No ... no-no ... *(Fumbling.)* Why don't I just sit here acting my age, quietly reading my paper till my wife comes? Tell you the truth, I've just had lunch and it makes me drowsy. *(Head raised, eyes shut.)* But I'll be okay in a minute ... *(Begins panting in anxiety.)*
CALVIN. I really don't mind, I like explaining, and I have a right to explain.
PETERS. *(Panting anxiously — nearly shouting.)* I respect your rights but whose nap is this? *(Breaks off.)*
CALVIN. It's why I've always felt just slightly ... you know ... under par.
PETERS. *(Anxiously.)* Oh no, Calvin, you mustn't say that; you don't look at all under par. In fact, I wish I looked as successful and vigorous and trustworthy as you.
CALVIN. But you are successful. Although I am, in my way.
PETERS. Of course you are. We're both equally successful and promising.
CALVIN. Yes. Although in a way, I am more.
PETERS. It's a relief to hear you say that.
CALVIN. You're relieved because it's not true.
PETERS. If you feel it's true, it's true.
CALVIN. I'd feel it more if it *was*. True, that is.
PETERS. We're depressing one another, don't you think? Why don't we both be quiet and, if necessary, just think about each other, okay? Sssh. Sssh. And maybe the time has come to for-

get this powder room. *(Sleeps, breathes deeply.)*
ADELE. Those toilet seats are solid African mahogany. Ask any detective — the imprint of woman's flesh on solid mahogany can never be entirely washed away.
PETERS. I can't bear not understanding this.
ADELE. Think of it — if science could come up with a way of reading those mahogany seats, we could identify women who went to their reward over a hundred years ago. We could inquire about their lives, their shoes and their deaths. When I enter that powder room it's like the silence of a cathedral, a place of remembrance where dead women linger. It's always three o'clock in the morning in that room, and thoughts come up from the depths. And the dusty oval mirrors still reflect the forgotten beauty of long-departed women in their sweeping satin gowns.
PETERS. This fluency is alarming — can they all be dying? *(Larry Tedesco enters.)*
CALVIN. Yes? Can I help you?
LARRY. I'm from Posito's. *(Indicates.)* The shoe store?
PETERS. *(Sits up.)* Yes! — I was just in there, you sold me these shoes! *(Raises a foot.)* Quadruple-A! *(Alarmed.)* My God, I paid you, didn't I?
LARRY. *(To Calvin.)* My wife come in here?
PETERS. *(To himself.)* But he can't be dead, he just sold me these ... *(Breaks off, looking at his shoes, then looks about.)* Listen, please — these are real shoes! I paid with money! *(To Larry.)* Or rather a credit card, didn't I?
LARRY. You got some kind a problem?
PETERS. *(Intimidated.)* No. No problem.
CALVIN. Do I know your wife?
LARRY. *(Suspiciously.)* I wouldn't be surprised; I'll look around, okay?
CALVIN. Go ahead, but I don't know what she'd be legitimately doing in here; you can see for yourself, it's all torn apart.
LARRY. *(Indicates off.)* Okay?
CALVIN. But what would she be doing here?
LARRY. *(Shrugs — not saying.)* You mind?

PETERS.   Please let this man look for his wife, if he loves her he might hear her call and jump into the water and save us all!
CALVIN.   *(To Larry.)* Well, okay, go ahead. But no fooling around back there, wife or no wife, got it? *(Larry saunters off. — Suggestive sneer.)* You know that broad?
PETERS.   Me? *(Embarrassed.)* I've never been in this neighborhood before. Not that I'm trying to deny her — she's very lovely, I say that openly.
CALVIN.   She's juicy. A prime sirloin. A ripe pomegranate. A Spanish blood orange. An accordion-pleated fuck.
PETERS.   *(Recalling.)* Yes, I know, but please; I hate talking like this about a woman behind her back ...
CALVIN.   What's the difference? — she'll never know.
PETERS.   Why won't she? Oh! You mean ... *(Breaks off.)* Oh ...
CALVIN.   All her underwear has been sold, stolen, or given away. And the phones don't ring that deep.
PETERS.   Yes. I see. — And where she is...?
CALVIN.   She's nowhere.
PETERS.   Yes, but is she older now? Has she grown into herself at last? *(Cathy-May appears; in a middle-aged woman's coat.)* Glasses? *(She takes out a pair and puts them on.)* Would it be a little less angry between us now that she's complete and her fires are banked? *(She turns slowly to him. A calm, slow smile spreads across her face. He smiles back familiarly. They both rise.)* Oh yes, darling, smile ... do that! *(Music: a Big Band: "Just One of Those Things,"* or an equivalent. They dance close, the music speeds, they separate with hands clasped and when he moves to draw her back she disappears into darkness.)*
CALVIN.   Anyway, once upon a time this building was a bank.
PETERS.   *(Desperation.)* Oh don't, I beg you do not start explaining this building, will you? I'm too old for sad stories!
CALVIN.   Why sad? I'm telling about a bank!
PETERS.   Yes, but recalling a dead bank is painful. In those days ... in those days ... banks were built like fortresses, not salad bars. They had those gigantic, beautifully filigreed brass gates, and they did not go around shystering people, begging

---

* See Special Note on Songs and Recordings on copyright page.

them to borrow money. No, they sat behind their little brass grills and *suspected* you. So you had to be upright, honest and good or you were practically under arrest the minute you walked in from the street! And the clerks — what about their cute white blouses with those little rounded collars — You don't call it sad that all that is no more?

CALVIN. But think of the high-class ladies who used to come in to talk over their inheritance, and also, incidentally, to have a pee. And the dense perfumes those women wore! And the way they crossed and separated their legs!

PETERS. *(Clapping his ears shut.)* Stop it, I beg you!

CALVIN. Well then don't go on saying you have no interest in this place! Sooner or later, as I said, these rich ladies, after spending the afternoon shopping or having coffee or tea ...

PETERS. Or probably a sip of champagne ...

CALVIN. Right. They had to pee, so they stopped at the bank ... *(Peters sighs openly, rests head tiredly on hand.)* This is very important — As early as the turn of the century *(Peters stretches out in the chair, arm over his eyes.)* the women already held most of the money in this country. Probably all countries. Because they live longer. Because of the salads, in my opinion. Without women you could forget lettuce. *(Peters sleeps.)* Sir?

PETERS. *(Awakened.)* What? — Oh no, I enjoy salads, my father was Italian. Especially arugula and even some nice fresh spinach. My mother was Spanish as a matter of fact. God knows what I am anymore.

CALVIN. I personally crossed the river Don with two hundred pounds of the family silver under my shirt, I was twelve and very brave, and the weight built up my legs.

PETERS. None of that is true, is it.

CALVIN. Well in a way ...

PETERS. It's all right; it's just that you remind me of somebody who used to make up stories like that. But I can't remember who he was.

CALVIN. Then let's say it was me.

PETERS. Okay.

CALVIN. Look, you're not flying anywhere, are you?

PETERS. *(Sitting up.)* Flying! They haven't let me into a cock-

pit for eighteen years! I had at least five years of flying left in me when they dumped me like a bag of shit! And the Democrats are no better!
CALVIN. Then let me finish; this could soothe you, it's very educational.
PETERS. Is this the subject?
CALVIN. Let me finish.
PETERS. No! I have a right to know the subject! Precious days are passing! Hours! I will need this time!
CALVIN. After the bank it was a library. The Morris family, the largest privately-owned public library in America, I was told — the idea was to educate the working class.
PETERS. Whose idea? *(Quickly amending.)* — Unless you're not supposed to tell.
CALVIN. Rich people; they had ideas like that in those ancient times. You know — the Frick Museum, the Astor 42nd Street Library, Morgan, Rockefeller —
ADELE. Carnegie?
CALVIN. *(Reluctantly.)* Carnegie is correct.
ADELE. The Frick has very nice toilets too ... lots of marble.
CALVIN. Right. Those bastards stole but they gave back; now they steal and they fly the coop. And what's the answer? — religion; those old-time crooks were afraid of God. Anyway ...
PETERS. Not that I love the rich; in fact, between their greed and stupidity they wrecked the greatest airline in the world.
CALVIN. Are you serious?
PETERS. Am I serious! — For generations my family were the only chiropractors in Naples! One of them is buried in the marble floor of the cathedral; yes, and a yard away from the king ... who incidentally had terrible arthritis, so you'd think they'd have buried him in a warmer place.
CALVIN. I'm glad you're feeling better. Anyway, the Morris family died off and then you had the Depression and where you're sitting now was a cafeteria through the thirties. The famous Eagle Cafeteria, open twenty-four hours.
PETERS. *(Almost, not quite remembering.)* Ah yes! — where I'm sitting now. Philosophical Marxist discussions going through the night. Leon Trotsky was supposed to have been a waiter,

which I'd like to believe, but who ever heard of a waiter in a cafeteria? Anyway, the dates don't work out; by the thirties Trotsky was already the head of the Red Army —
CALVIN. So, that's more or less the history. Was that so bad?
PETERS. No-no, I'm beginning to enjoy it. Why don't you rest now, you must be pretty old, too, aren't you?
CALVIN. Me? I stopped getting old a long time ago. *(Pause.)*
PETERS. ... *Stopped getting old,* did you say? *(Calvin is silent, motionless, stares front. Something horrifying dawns on Peters.)* Ohhh ... *(Covers his face.)* Oh my God, yes! — Then where is this? Say, you're not all dead here, are you?
CALVIN. Don't let it bother you; life is one to a customer and no returns if you're not satisfied.
PETERS. Listen, I really have to leave; I don't belong here! Just because a man decides to buy a pair of quadruple-A shoes ... is that fair? *(Struggling to rise.)* I am leaving!
CALVIN. What will I do with your wife!
PETERS. My wife? Oh God, I don't know, just ... just ... kiss her and tell her ... to ... to ... sadly die. *(Peters lies back, falling asleep again.)*
CALVIN. — It's important to know that up until the Vietnam War the place was a real moneymaker, but those little fellas in their black pajamas killed all the nightclubs.
PETERS. Vietnamese killed the nightclubs?
CALVIN. Destroyed all the optimism. And the pessimism. No optimism, no clubs; no pessimism, no clubs.
PETERS. Then what's left?
CALVIN. Vacillation, indecision, self-satisfaction and religion — all enemies of nightclubs. In London, on the other hand ...
PETERS. Wait! Before you get to London ... could you give me an idea of the subject.
CALVIN. *(Angrily.)* I'm explaining — I said I don't mind.
PETERS. *(Desperately.)* I know you don't mind but I am not happy when I don't know even what the subject is! *(Shouting.)* Can't I have a hint! I ask you ... a hint! A hint!
CALVIN. *(Frustrated.)* For God's sake, man, they have clubs in London that go on for a hundred, two hundred years! Can you imagine anything like that here? Anyway, that's the history.

(Peters stands up, peers out in silence.) What is this misery of yours?
PETERS.   *(He softly sings the first line of a song, such as "I've got a crush on you, sweetie pie,"* or another from the same era. Sings another line, then it dies.)* You're not from Moscow, by any chance?
CALVIN.   Odessa. Name a great violinist and you can bet he came from Odessa. I'm talking Mischa Ellman, I'm talking Sasha Schneider, and Misha Auer ...
PETERS.   Misha Auer did not come from Odessa, but that's all right.
CALVIN.   Well, the greatest olives in the world come from Odessa.
PETERS.   It's all right, just go on lying, why shouldn't you? Is it believable that during the war I delivered our P-40 fighter planes to Odessa? I had some great hopes for Russia then, but terribly puritanical — I inadvertently learned you must never get into bed with two Russian women. And incidentally, every adventurous woman I met there carried a bathtub stopper in her purse.
CALVIN.   I was never conservative enough to be a communist. Seriously — soon as a girl joined the party she'd cross her unshaven legs and you might as well go to the library.
PETERS.   *(Sits.)* I think the subject is — humiliation. Give up the gin, then the vermouth and end up having to explain to a Princeton class which war you were in. Talk about futility. Christ's sake, behind our propellers we were saving the world! And now, "which war ..." So you end up staring into space, with maybe some woman's wonderful ass floating by, or a banana split. Remember banana splits; four balls of ice cream on a sliced banana, covered with hand-whipped cream, chocolate sauce and a maraschino cherry on top ... for twenty-five cents? That, my friend, was a country, huh? I mean *that was a country!* — And who ever had a key to their front door?
CALVIN.   Unheard of. You said you had a question?
PETERS.   A question? Oh yes, yes ... *(Takes out a tabloid paper.)*

---

* See Special Note on Songs and Recordings on copyright page.

Why are you so untruthful? Are you trying to destroy the world?
CALVIN.   Destroy the world! — I'm just talking!
PETERS.   *(Springing up.)* That's it!! That's what I think I've been trying to say since I walked in here! — "Just talking" is ... is ... There is no subject anymore! Turn on the radio, turn on the television, what is it — just talking! It can sink the ship! *(Breaks off, bewildered. Gripping his forehead.)* Something's happening to me.
CALVIN.   Something like what?
PETERS.   *(Holds up his paper as though just discovering it in hand.)* ... I found this on the train. Amazing ads; pages and pages ... look; breast augmentation, $4,400. And guess how much breast reduction is.
CALVIN.   How much?
PETERS.   Same price. That seem strange to you?
CALVIN.   ... No, seems about right.
PETERS.   My father paid five thousand for the eight-room house our whole family lived in for thirty years! And a pair of tits is five thousand?
CALVIN.   Yes. But houses are not as important; put a house on one magazine cover and a pair of tits on another, which one'll sell?
PETERS.   And here we have penile augmentation for four thousand dollars and hymen reconstruction for two thousand. I can't imagine why hymens are cheaper.
CALVIN.   There's not as much to a hymen. And they're nothing but trouble.
PETERS.   Ah! But isn't it odd that penile augmentation costs four hundred dollars *less* than breast augmentation.
CALVIN.   Well, I wouldn't take it personally.
PETERS.   *(Turning pages.)* But you have to, don't you?! I read these ads and I wonder — "Why don't I understand this?" You see? WHY DON'T I UNDERSTAND THIS! *(A sudden quizzical expression.)* Please don't be offended, but are you asleep?
CALVIN.   Me? *(Larry reenters.)*
LARRY.   Thanks. If you see her let me know, would you? I'm Larry, in Posito's near the corner.

CALVIN. What's she look like?
LARRY. What she looks like? ... She looks perfect. With a white angora sweater. And pink, plastic, spike-heel shoes. A little on the pudgy side but not too fat ... just ... you know, perfect.
PETERS. What made you think she would be in here?
LARRY. *(He shrugs.)* She could be. *(Nods.)* She could be anywhere. The neighborhood's got a lot of Jews, you know. And Koreans now and Chinks.
PETERS. *(In Italian.) E Italiani.*
LARRY. I'm Italian.
PETERS. *(In Italian.) Certo; non sonno sordo? (In English.)* You know, Larry, Italians have always been a tolerant people.
LARRY. Fuck that, sir.
PETERS. Excuse me but "fuck that, sir" is not a way to talk intelligently. Italian tolerance comes from the Roman era when so many different races flooded into the empire ... Arabs, Gauls, Spanish, Nordics, Russians ...
CALVIN. Lithuanians.
PETERS. *(Sharply.)* Not Lithuanians.
LARRY. In March the niggers busted our window, robbed forty-one pairs of shoes.
CALVIN. I heard about that.
LARRY. You heard about it? We're fed up. Fed up!
ADELE. Us too.
LARRY. I didn't hear that. *(Leaning angrily toward Peters.)* Fuck the tolerance, sir, that's all over. Finished! Now we protect ourselves! *(To Calvin.)* Thanks. *(To Peters.)* Good luck with the shoes. By the way, her name is Cathy; Cathy-May.
PETERS. Yes, I know ... But is she the same Cathy-May who used to be alive? — I don't mean "alive" in that sense, I mean ... *(Larry exits. Peters leans his elbows on his thighs and holds his head in despair.)* It didn't used to get to me — but lately ... almost every time I take my nap ... it's like a long icicle slowly stabbing down into my balls.
CALVIN. When I lived in Florence ...
PETERS. *(Open fury.)* For God's sake, don't say one additional thing, will you?! *(Eyes shut, hand on forehead.)* I wonder if I'm eating too much for lunch. *(Suddenly turning on Adele.)* Excuse me,

but may I ask what you are doing here?

ADELE. *(She puts on a nurse's cap.)* Thank you for your interest. With God's permission I live here. I hope none of you has the idea of tearing this building down.

PETERS. Why are you putting on a nurse's cap?

ADELE. Could it be I'm a nurse? And before you mock me, be sure you don't get sick and need my services.

PETERS. I'm not at all mocking you, but a nurse sitting around drinking like that ...

ADELE. You mock everyone! Look at how you mocked that handsome shoe salesman!

PETERS. But it's a mistake, she can't have married a lout like him! She's not really a common slut, you know — and she's ... well I won't say she's ... *(A choked cry.)* She's dead? *(A realization.)* Or not? ... Not? *(High hope suddenly.)* Please! Is she? What is her situation!

ADELE. I'm not a nurse; sorry.

PETERS. Then what are you doing with that cap!

ADELE. I just found it on the sidewalk outside the Lenox Hill Hospital, probably some nurse lost it jumping into a cab to meet her date, probably a well-to-do elderly man who was going to fix her up for life. But if I was a nurse would I have the right to sit around drinking booze?

PETERS. Of course, just as he ... *(To Calvin.)* I've forgotten, what was your right...? *(Leonard and Rose enter. He carries a guitar case. He is holding her by the elbow.)*

LEONARD. Excuse me, can she sit down?

CALVIN. We're closed. We only open the second floor around six-thirty.

LEONARD. She's pregnant.

CALVIN. Oh! Well, have a chair. They've all been reglued. *(Leonard and Calvin quickly seat her.)*

ROSE. *(Sitting.)* Don't worry, I'm not having it, I just walked too much.

CALVIN. Relax, we're all on the side of the pregnant woman. *(Asking.)* You're not the father.

LEONARD. How'd you know!

CALVIN. What's to know? — nobody's the father anymore.

(To Peters.) So that's the history. *(To Rose.)* If you need the powder room, it's straight that way.

ROSE. Thank you, I will in a minute.

LEONARD. I've passed this place a hundred times and never knew it was a nightclub ... it is, isn't it?

CALVIN. That's our style, or it was — no sign outside, no advertising; people either want to be here or they don't. Most didn't, obviously. *(To Peters.)* I'll be in my office if your wife is interested. *(Slows beside Rose.)* I hope you know the father.

ROSE. Of course I know the father!

PETERS. Of course!

CALVIN. Just kidding — it's only that they used to say — I'm talking forty, fifty years ago — "A man who betrays his wife will betray his country."

PETERS. *(Simultaneously.)* "... Will betray his country."

CALVIN. I figured you knew that saying.

PETERS. Haven't heard it in fifty years, and it's still idiotic. What has screwing a woman got to do with betraying your country?

CALVIN. Nothing, but nobody even *says* things like that anymore. *(To Rose.)* Morals count, you know, even if you just say them. *(Making to leave.)* Excuse me, Professor.

PETERS. How did you know I was a professor?

CALVIN. What else could you be? — I can smell the chalk. *(Touching his temple.)* Nobody forgets chalk. *(He exits. Peters stares after him, perplexed, deeply curious. Silence. Rose takes out a bottle of Evian and drinks. Finally.)*

PETERS. How old are you people now, if you don't mind my asking?

LEONARD. I'm twenty-seven.

ROSE. Twenty-eight now.

ADELE. *(Unasked.)* Thirty-four.

PETERS. And you're all ... *(Embarrassed chuckle.)* I feel a little funny asking, but ... you're all awake, aren't you.

ROSE. Awake?

PETERS. Forget it. Maybe it's that I don't see many young people anymore, so it's hard to guess their ages ... To me, everybody looks about twenty-two. Do you find it hard to follow what people are saying?

LEONARD. Well ... not really. *(To Rose.)* Do we? *(Before she can answer.)* Except she never listens anyway.
ROSE. I do listen, but I have my own thoughts and it's hard to listen while I'm thinking.
PETERS. Let me put it another way — Do you find you get sleepy after lunch, or when do you start?
ADELE. Getting sleepy? The minute I wake up.
PETERS. It struck me the other day that everyone I know is sleepy, — I wonder if it's something about the times.
ROSE. Maybe you're low on potassium. You should eat bananas.
PETERS. I do eat two or three a week for breakfast. Actually I rather like bananas.
ROSE. You should try to love them. Motivation is important in the diet; bananas are there to be loved. Try eating five a week. Seven or eight would be even better. Or ten.
PETERS. Isn't that quite a lot of bananas?
ROSE. *(She raises one leg in a stretch.)* You only have enough bananas when one more would make you want to throw up. I know about such things, I'm a dancer, dancers need trace elements for the knees.
PETERS. *Trace elements for the knees?*
ROSE. They're tiny but important.
PETERS. *(Nods with a certain alarm.) Trace elements for the knees?* You see, this is what I mean; when I was young no human being from one end of the United States to the other would have uttered that sentence. For example, my father and grandfather — I don't recall them ever in the presence of a banana. And they lived into their nineties.
ADELE. Same thing with my mother; she can gross down two, three at a time, a woman over ninety and no bigger than a thimble and still driving an eight-cylinder Buick loaded with extras — air bags, defrosting side mirrors, tinted glass ... *(Continues mouthing.)*
PETERS. In fact, nobody ate bananas when I was young. You make me wonder how we managed.
ADELE. ... Fifteen-inch wheels, leather trim, non-skid brakes, moon roof, lighted trunk ... *(Continues mouthing.)*
ROSE. People had different thoughts then, and there was

nothing around to get them so exhausted.

ADELE. Upholstered armrest, front and rear utility lights, metallic paint ... V6, three-and-a-half-litre engine, automatic transmission ... *(Goes on mouthing.)*

PETERS. *(Nods in silence for a moment.)* Please forgive my curiosity, but does this conversation revolve around some ... subject that I am unaware of?

LEONARD. A subject? I don't think so ... *(To Rose.)* Does it?

ROSE. What? Excuse me, I was thinking of something.

LEONARD. You know, darling, it's not very polite to drop out of a conversation without telling anybody.

PETERS. Unless we don't need a subject anymore. *(They look at him blankly.)* I mean do you people ever wonder ... as you're getting into bed, what you were talking about all day?

LEONARD. I don't think so. *(To Rose.)* Do we?

ROSE. When we're getting into *bed?*

PETERS. Or for example, I do enjoy the movies, but every so often I wonder, "What was the *subject* of the picture?"

ROSE. The subject of a *picture?*

PETERS. I remember my mother — washing machines were rather rare in those times — and she'd have the maid boil the sheets and the laundry on the stove and lug it all up to the roof of the apartment house to dry. Have you ever heard of that?

ROSE. Boiling sheets?

LEONARD. On a gas stove? That's a fire hazard!

ROSE. Water is fireproof, Leonard.

PETERS. *(Forcing concentration; peering.)* No-no, I think what I'm trying to ... to ... find my connection with is a ... what's the word ... *continuity* ... yes, with the past, perhaps ... in the hope of finding a ... yes, a subject. That's the idea, I think, but I'm exhausted ...

ROSE. Boiling sheets?

LEONARD. But that's not really a *subject.*

ROSE. Well then, going up to the roof?

PETERS. That's it! Yes! Maybe!

ROSE. But wouldn't wet sheets weigh a ton?

PETERS. Right! And nobody would do that anymore! So maybe that's a real subject, because one thing reveals another.

What else about that?

ROSE.   Maybe that's why you need more bananas now.

PETERS.   *(To Leonard.)* Say now! She makes a lot of sense! You've relieved me a lot.

ROSE.   Really? Why?

PETERS.   Because you have added to what I said! Rather than exhausting me by starting a whole new unrelated conversation. That's really glorious! Thank you so much. *(Tears flow, he wipes them.)*

ROSE.   Don't be upset.

PETERS.   It's just that when you've flown into hundreds of gorgeous sunsets, you want them to go on forever and ever ... and hold off the darkness ... *(The trumpet plays a loud blast of "My Blue Heaven,"* or an equivalent. His anxiety soars.)* How like sex the trumpet is — it always leaves you kind of sad when it's finished. You know, every spring ... every spring the Polish maids would carry our carpets up to the roof and hang them out on wires, and they'd beat them for hours until their blouses were dark with sweat. When April came and early May, hundreds of rooftops all over the city had those big fair-haired Polish girls walloping clouds of carpet dust to drift out over the avenues.

ROSE.   Was this before vacuum cleaners?

PETERS.   *(Frowning, disturbed, he pants.)* Oh, God, imagine dying in the midst of a conversation about vacuum cleaners!

LEONARD.   *(Passionately.)* But would it be any better talking about differential calculus? The thing is not to be afraid ...

ROSE.   *(She covers his hand.)* That's right, dear.

PETERS.   But you're so young — how can you know!

LEONARD.   We're afraid.

PETERS.   Oh, good, then we can talk without my risking your disdain — yes, we did have a vacuum cleaner; but it screamed like a coal truck and it frightened the Polish girls. Actually, though, I think it was virtue that made people go lugging those carpets up to the roof. Discomfort was righteous in America; when Teddy Roosevelt went sweating through the jungle hunt-

---

* See Special Note on Songs and Recordings on copyright page.

ing tigers he wore a tie; Woodrow Wilson, Warren Harding, Calvin Coolidge, Herbert Hoover — those men went fishing in the same itchy dark suits they wore at their inaugurations; they waded into wild rivers wearing cuff links, stiff collars and black high-topped shoes. The President of the United States was above all morally righteous, you see, rather than just entertaining. Even after President Harding was exposed as the father of an illegitimate daughter he continued to take precisely the same virtuous photographs. And Grover Cleveland likewise. And for that matter, George Washington was in and out of so many beds they finally called him the father of his country. But no one ever questioned his dignity, you see. Or his virtue. And he was never exhausted. I can't remember my point.
ROSE. I definitely think something very tiring is in the air now.
LEONARD. It's lead. *(All turn to him.)* It's a proven fact, there's more lead than ever in the air.
PETERS. But we seem to be living longer than ever.
LEONARD. But in a poisoned condition.
ROSE. Like you being so sleepy. You might live to a hundred, but half asleep.
LEONARD. You know? — I just realized — I've been getting up later and later in the mornings.
ROSE. Maybe you're just a teeny bit depressed, Leonard. *(She kisses his cheek lightly.)*
ADELE. Depression'll do it every time.
LEONARD. Like do you find you're a little more slow-witted than you used to be?
ADELE. You can count me in there.
PETERS. Definitely, yes. But couldn't it be this constant changing of the subject that's wearing out our brains?
LEONARD. *(To Rose. Indicating Peters.)* Sounds like lead. You know the Romans used lead pipes in their water systems and also wine storage, and one emperor after another was nutty as a fruitcake.
ROSE. And lots of subnormal children.
LEONARD. The Teutonic tribes, on the other hand ...
PETERS. *(Gripping his forehead.)* Would you mind not talking about the Teutonic tribes? —

LEONARD.   It's just that they drank out of lakes and clear streams ...
PETERS.   Yes, I know, but I am much older than I look and there is just so much irrelevant information that I am able to ...
LEONARD.   But everything is relevant! If you don't mind my saying it, that's what you don't seem to understand and what is making you rather pessimistic. You are trying to pick and choose what is important, sir, like a batter waiting for a ball he can hit. But what if you have to happily swing at everything they throw at you? The fact is — those Germanic tribes were drinking fresh water and came down and just wiped out the Roman Empire! Which was drinking wine loaded with lead! I think that's kind of relevant, isn't it? Incidentally, we never picked up the laundry. Or maybe wait till tomorrow?
ROSE.   There's still time. Where'd he say that powder room was?
PETERS.   That way, I believe, in the back. *(Rose exits.)*
LEONARD.   *(Calling after her.)* Maybe I should try to pick it up now? *(To Peters.)* I just hate leaving laundry overnight. On the other hand, I've never lost any. Although I did get a wrong shirt once. *(Getting up to leave.)* Maybe tell her I left, would you? — Well, never mind, I'll wait. *(Sits again.)* Except one of those shirts belongs to my brother, it's very expensive. I'd better go. *(Stands.)* ... Well, I'll wait, to hell with it, he's got fifty shirts. *(Sits. Pause.)*
PETERS.   You may have read the Babylonian myth explaining why there are so many different languages in the world?
LEONARD.   No.
PETERS.   God was extremely annoyed by the racket in the streets, so he invented all the different languages to keep people from talking to each other so much.
LEONARD.   That's pretty funny.
PETERS.   Are you in business?
LEONARD.   No, I'm a composer. And investor.
ADELE.   You may as well ask why I started drinking.
PETERS.   *(A bare glance at Adele.)* Then what are you doing here?

LEONARD. My friend had to urinate.
PETERS. Of course! — My God, I think I'm just swinging at random from limb to limb.
LEONARD. Are you in business?
PETERS. No, I flew for Pan Am for many years, then some lecturing at Princeton till I retired.
LEONARD. May I ask your subject?
PETERS. Oh, mysterious things — like the suicidal impulse in large corporations. Are you a college man?
LEONARD. Harvard, yes.
PETERS. Well, that's not a bad school. Incidentally, are you asleep? I only ask because it just occurs to me that I may be awake. *(Chuckles.)* ... Horrible as that would be. But that's impossible, isn't it — a person awake can't talk to one who's asleep. You are, aren't you — asleep? But that's not right either, is it; two sleeping people can't converse can they. *(Chuckles.)* You can't share sleep, can you. Any more than death, right? So ... I'm asleep. But you — what's your ... you know ... situation? What bothers me is that — look at these shoes; they're obviously brand-new, right? *(Leonard looks at them.)* So all this must be happening, right? I didn't produce these shoes out of thin air, correct? Look at the soles ... not even soiled. *(Leonard looks at soles, but almost deanimatedly, totally uninterested.)* And I couldn't have bought them in my sleep, could I. You walk into a store with your eyes closed they're not going to let you walk out with a new pair of shoes ... What's begun to haunt me is that next to nothing I have believed has turned out to be true. *(Breaks off in a surge of fear.)* IF SHE DOESN'T COME, DOES IT MEAN I CAN'T LEAVE?! WHERE IS MY POOR GODDAMNED WIFE! *(On the verge of weeping, the piano plays loud and fast, for a moment — "If You Knew Suzie,"* and stops.)*
LEONARD. Is she ill?
PETERS. We are both ill; we are sick of each other. *(Shouts.)* Her imagination is destroying me! *(Moment.)* We're happy. *(Takes a few deep breaths.)* — I'm much obliged to you for listening. Are you Jewish?

---

* See Special Note on Songs and Recordings on copyright page.

LEONARD. Yes.
PETERS. I thought so; Jews and Italians are happy to allow a person to mourn.
ADELE. Yes, we cry them into the grave.
PETERS. Tell me ... this Calvin guy here ... the owner or manager or whatever he is ... Did you notice anything odd about his eyes?
LEONARD. His eyes? *(A moment; thinks.)* Say now ... yes. It's almost like ... I can't describe it, almost like there's nothing in his eye sockets. No! — it's that his eyes ... can it be they have no color? *(Peters stares, silent.)* Is that what you mean? *(Peters says nothing.)* What is it, some disease?
PETERS. *(Motionless.)* He's my brother.
LEONARD. Your brother! Did you know he was here?
PETERS. Oh no, no, it just came to me. *(Pause.)* He's dead. *(Leonard astonished.)* Drowned almost twenty years ago.
LEONARD. You mean he's *like* your brother.
PETERS. *(Shakes his head.)* No. *(Leonard is silent, terrified.)* His eyes ... they're almost translucent, like jellyfish; the sea in winter; the insides of oyster shells ...
LEONARD. Well, I ... I don't know what to say ... Does he know you're his brother?
PETERS. I'm not sure. It's hard to know how much the dead remember, isn't it ... But that's not quite right ... *(Stares in silence, smiles now.)*
LEONARD. I understand.
PETERS. ... You see, he was always a great kidder and practical joker. Once he was driving us down the Rocky Mountains and pretended the brakes had failed. Darn near a hundred miles an hour and heading straight for the rail when he pretended the brakes came back. A cruel streak, but full of life.
LEONARD. You mean he pretended to drown, as a joke?
PETERS. I'm wondering that. He was capable of anything. But that can't be right, we were all at his funeral. — I'm wondering if my wife got lost. Could you be a good fellow and take a look outside? She's very short ... although you might not agree ...
LEONARD. *(Gets up.)* What's her name?
PETERS. Her name? *(Touches his head.)* I'm so embarrassed.

LEONARD. Well it doesn't matter ...
PETERS. Oh it does, it does! — What I do in these circumstances is start with A and go down the alphabet. Anna, Annabella, Augusta, Bernice, Beatrice ...
LEONARD. Well what's your name ... just so I can approach her. *(Peters stares in deepening anxiety.)* It's all right, I'll just look for a short woman ...
PETERS. It's not all right! *(Suddenly.)* Charlotte! Charlotte Peters! — My God this is terrible.
LEONARD. No-no, maybe I shouldn't have asked ...
PETERS. This is the worst I've had. It's not Alzheimer's, I've been examined ... I wonder if it's just a case of not wanting to be around anymore.
LEONARD. I'd look into lead.
PETERS. Oh, my boy, I wish it were lead, but in the end I'm afraid one arrives at a sort of terminal indifference, and there is more suspense in the bowel movement than a Presidential election.
LEONARD. But I often forget things ... In fact, as a child I used to wonder why we needed to remember at all. Wouldn't it be wonderful if we got up in the morning and everyone was a complete stranger?
PETERS. Are your parents divorced?
LEONARD. Yes, that's where I got the idea. Do you think things are worse than years ago? — Although I'm glad there's penicillin.
PETERS. Penicillin is definitely better, yes, but things have been getting worse since Eden; it's not lead, however.
LEONARD. What then?
PETERS. Washington, Jefferson ... most of the founding fathers were all Deists, you know; they believed that God had wound up the world like a clock and then disappeared. We are unwinding now, the ticks are further and further apart. So instead of tick-tick-tick-tick-tick we've got tick *(Pause.)* tick *(Pause.)* tick. And we get bored between ticks, and boredom is a form of dying, and dying, needless to say, takes an awful lot out of a person.
LEONARD. But so many things are happening.

PETERS. But not the main thing. The main thing is emphatically not happening at all and probably never will again.
LEONARD. And what is that?
PETERS. Redemption.
LEONARD. I've never really understood that word.
PETERS. That's all right, no one understands love either, but look how we long for it.
LEONARD. Then you believe in God?
PETERS. I'm quite sure I do, yes.
LEONARD. What would you say God is? Or is that too definite?
PETERS. Not at all — God is precisely what is not there when you need him. And what work of beauty have you created this week?
LEONARD. I haven't done much this week.
PETERS. Well, I suppose that can happen in the creative life.
LEONARD. I'm not having much of a creative life these days.
PETERS. Lover trouble?
LEONARD. As a matter of fact, I recently split up with somebody.
PETERS. Too bad. Boy or girl?
LEONARD. Girl.
PETERS. Well, cheer up and pray that you run into a girl who makes you imagine you've forgotten the other fifty million single American women walking around loose. — Charlotte! Here I am! *(He has spotted his wife. She enters, looking all around.)*
CHARLOTTE. For Christ's sake.
PETERS. Yes, it's pretty awful.
CHARLOTTE. Awful! — it's marvelous! Look at those moldings, look at that ceiling, look at these floors. Gimme a break, this is heaven! *(Rose enters.)* And who is this lovely young pregnant woman? *(Rose looks at Charlotte and laughs.)*
LEONARD. She's not so short.
CHARLOTTE. *(To Peters.)* What is this again?
PETERS. *(Covering his eyes.)* I'm terribly sorry, I had a vision of you as being quite ...
CHARLOTTE. He said I was *short*?
LEONARD. *(To Peters.)* I'm awfully sorry! *(To Charlotte.)* He

asked me to go out and look for you and he couldn't think of your name, so he ...
CHARLOTTE. *(Laughing angrily; to Peters.)* Couldn't think of my *name!*
LEONARD. *(Tortured.)* Only for a minute!
CHARLOTTE. In my opinion it's his flying for three solid years in World War II; the Essex Class Carrier had a very short flight deck and it blew his nerves. *(To Peters.)* I'll bet something here reminded you of the war, didn't it.
PETERS. ... As a matter of fact ... *(Looking around.)* ... I think I said this place could use a small bomb.
CHARLOTTE. There you go. — Where's this Mister Calvin?
PETERS. He said he'd be in his office if you were interested. He said you should see the powder room.
CHARLOTTE. Gimme a break — the *powder* room?
ROSE. It's glorious. I was just in there — I've never been like ... kissed by a room, or felt such good-hearted *safety,* or like a room was hugging me. It's like you suddenly didn't have to ... like defend yourself. It's a sort of *courteous* room, you know? I mean the energy I use up just keeping people from ... *bothering* me, you know what I mean?
CHARLOTTE. I know exactly what you mean, I'm a decorator.
LEONARD. Really! — we were just thinking of calling a decorator for her apartment.
ROSE. But it's so tiny ... practically a closet.
PETERS. It doesn't matter, if it's vertical she'll happily decorate it.
CHARLOTTE. You're not the father?
PETERS. They're only friends. He just brought her in here to pee.
CHARLOTTE. He did? Well, that is one of the most encouraging things I've heard in I don't know how long. — I must have a look at this powder room.
ROSE. It's straight that way. Watch out for the lumber on the floor.
CHARLOTTE. I know how you feel, we have four daughters. All four are flight attendants on major airlines.
PETERS. *(To Leonard.)* I truly wonder whether the country

could be saved if people could stay on the same subject for more than twenty seconds.
CHARLOTTE.   So if you're planning on flying anywhere let us know and one of the girls might be able to look after you. Now let's see this famous powder room. *(She exits.)*
ROSE.   Actually, I was thinking of flying to Oregon to see a friend; maybe I could have one of your daughters' phone numbers.
PETERS.   *(Chuckling.)* I'm afraid the girls are not connected to the airlines.
LEONARD.   But didn't she say...?
PETERS.   Sometimes she is simply overwhelmed by a burst of comprehensive enthusiasm. A little like heels and skirts — one year high, next year low. Women have visions. Now, she has a vision of our four young women in those snug uniforms and cute little hats, feeding the multitudes. She's a very emotional woman, as you know by now, and she means no harm, but she has powerful longings.
LEONARD.   *(To Rose.)* That's really weird.
ROSE.   I don't know. I mean here I'm carrying around this, I assume, baby which could end up not even liking me ...
LEONARD.   Rose, how can you say a thing like that?
ROSE.   But how many of our friends really like their parents?
LEONARD.   Parents!
ROSE.   Yes! I'm going to be a *parent*, Leonard.
LEONARD.   Oh, right. *(Stares, shaking his head in amazement.)* This is turning out to be a really strange day. *(Charlotte enters; inspired, amazed.)*
CHARLOTTE.   Wow. Did you see it?
PETERS.   I don't normally go into powder rooms.
CHARLOTTE.   *(Pointing off imperiously.)* Go. GO!
PETERS.   I absolutely refuse! I have no conceivable interest in ...
CHARLOTTE.   Gimme a break, Harry, I insist you see that powder room! Now will you or won't you!
PETERS.   *(Rising.)* But I have no viewpoint toward powder rooms!
CHARLOTTE.   Well how about participating for once *without*

a viewpoint! I mean gimme a break, Harry, be human, this place is fantastic!
PETERS. *(Peering into air.)* I simply don't understand anything anymore. When I woke up this morning, I did not plan to shop for shoes, and I certainly did not expect to end the day inspecting a ladies' bathroom. *(To Leonard.)* Would you mind? — I'd like another man with me.
CHARLOTTE.   Oh, Harry darling, aren't you feeling well?
PETERS.   Let me put it this way ... *(He begins to weep.)* Are you feeling well, Charlotte?
CHARLOTTE.   I'm feeling wonderful.
PETERS.   I'm so glad for you. *(To Rose.)* She's everybody's mother ... as I'm sure you realize, and her happiness ... *(Sighs.)* is inexhaustible. *(Peters turns and goes, taking out a handkerchief as he exits.)*
LEONARD.   *(As he goes.)* I'm worried about my brother's shirt.
ROSE.   Leonard please, try to have some faith, it's only away in the laundry for the afternoon. Maybe think of it like a vacation it's on. *(Leonard exits following Peters.)*
CHARLOTTE.   How far along?
ROSE.   Six weeks, I think.
CHARLOTTE.   Did you want it or...?
ROSE.   *(Shrugs.)* It wants me, I know that much.
CHARLOTTE.   You sound alone.
ROSE.   I am, I guess. He can't quite make up his mind.
CHARLOTTE.   Men! If they were in charge of the sun it would go up and down every ten minutes. What happened! — a good man is so hard to find anymore.
ROSE.   My friend Leonard thinks it's something in the water.
CHARLOTTE.   He's not the father?
ROSE.   Sometimes he seems to think he is. But sometimes he doesn't.
CHARLOTTE.   What stories the world is full of! So are you telling him he is or he isn't?
ROSE.   I want to see what it looks like first.
CHARLOTTE.   Why! Tell him it's his and you can change your mind later.
ROSE.   But we always end up fighting like brother and sister.

And that can't be right, can it.
CHARLOTTE. You young people — why are you always digging away at each other for the truth? We never dreamed of telling the truth to a husband and the result was practically no divorces. — Well, thank God for the airlines! You know, if something drops on the uniform the company pays the cleaning.
ROSE. *(Near tears.)* How can you be so happy! — you're wonderful!
CHARLOTTE. I can't help myself — I've been happy since I was a baby and I never changed. It irritates my husband but what can I do? — First thing in the morning I open my eyes and I'm so overjoyed I could eat the whole world for breakfast. Listen, I like your Leonard; I would let him be the father.
ROSE. It's strange, I think I feel older than you.
CHARLOTTE. Italians love to cook, that's my salvation. And I'm in pretty fair shape — I used to dance, you know.
ROSE. Professionally?
CHARLOTTE. Radio City Rockettes nine years. We met in the alley of the theatre. He was a Navy pilot, stage-door Johnnie, he'd come back from bombing Asia and go banging through that chorus line ... eighteen girls on a thirty-day leave! But a delight, a dee-light! Funny? Gimme a break, the man was sheer humongous wit. I weighed one-eighteen those days, till the bread did me in. I lost twelve pounds last year but who's kidding who, I'm still everybody's mother. *(Leonard and Peters enter; rather expressionless, even solemn looks.)* Well? *(The men glance uneasily at one another.)* So? *(They still hesitate.)*
LEONARD. Well it's a washroom, right?
CHARLOTTE. A *washroom!*
PETERS. Where you wash up.
CHARLOTTE. *Mama mia ... (To Rose.)* They don't see anything! He walks around the house like a blind man — "Where's my glasses? Where's my suspenders? Where's my bathrobe?"
ROSE. By the way, how did you know I was pregnant?
CHARLOTTE. I'm part Gypsy.
LEONARD. *(To Peters.)* Is that true? *(Peters sighs and looks away.)*
CHARLOTTE. What does he know? To him nothing is true unless you can hammer it, fuck it or fly it around. — Gypsy

women, darling, can tell you're pregnant just by looking into your eyes. Not only that, but I can tell you it's a girl.
PETERS. Now how could you know *that*, for God's sake?
CHARLOTTE. Because the air is full of *things! (Gesturing between Rose and herself.)* And we are looking at each other through the air, aren't we?
PETERS. I feel I have lived my life and I eagerly look forward to a warm oblivion.
LEONARD. May I ask whether you intend to start a new nightclub or is this a...?
CHARLOTTE. Depends; if this man's deal is good I would certainly consider a new club ... why?
LEONARD. I'm not trying to pressure you but if it's going to be a club I'd like to talk to you about the music.
ROSE. He has a great little band. She danced in Radio City.
LEONARD. Really, a Rockette? *(To Peters.)* Is that true?
CHARLOTTE. Why do you keep asking him if it's true! You think I'm off my nut, or something?
LEONARD. Oh no-no, please don't think I ...
ROSE. No-no! He didn't mean anything like that ...
CHARLOTTE. *(To Peters.)* Well aren't you going to answer him?
PETERS. *(Shuts his eyes, sighs, then.)* Yes, it's true.
CHARLOTTE. Well I'll go find this Calvin and see what kind of deal he has in mind. Tell them your philosophy. *(Charlotte exits.)*
LEONARD. We should really pick up the laundry ...
ROSE. Your philosophy?
PETERS. No-no, it was only a dream I had many years ago. After my wing was destroyed.
ROSE. I love dreams, could you tell it?
PETERS. I'm afraid I have to rest now. Why don't we all?
ROSE. I'd love to, frankly. What was your dream?
LEONARD. Shouldn't I pick up the laundry?
ROSE. Try to rest, Leonard.
LEONARD. Should you be on the floor?
ROSE. It's okay.
LEONARD. Should I look for a pillow?
ROSE. You've got to try to have a little confidence, Leonard.

LEONARD. *(Self-blame.)* I know.
ROSE. I mean try to assume that whatever is going on out there will go on without us for a while. So you might as well rest.
ADELE. This is my kinda thing, I tell ya. It's been going on without me for a long, long time.
ROSE. All right then ... *(She stretches her legs. All lean back and close their eyes. Pause.)* I don't think you're resting, are you?
LEONARD. I want to be the father, Rose.
ROSE. We'll see. I don't like deciding right now.
LEONARD. But when you do, will you think of me?
ROSE. Of course. *(Slight pause.)* If not, you could be its brother.
LEONARD. A brother twenty-eight years older?
ROSE. Well, an older brother. It happens.
ADELE. Appearance is everything; my older sister's got those hips, those eyes and those ambitious legs — the girl could raise a man from the dead just by stepping over his grave. And now she's down Wall Street with her own office at Bear Stearns.
PETERS. I dreamed of another planet; it was very beautiful — the air was rose, the ground was beige, the water was green, the sky was the fairest blue. And the people were full of affection and respect, and then suddenly they grabbed a few defectives and flung them into space.
LEONARD. Why were they defective?
PETERS. They were full of avarice and greed. And they broke into thousands of pieces and fell to earth, and it is from their seed that we all descend.
LEONARD. Well that's very strange ... I mean we usually assume that man is born good ...
PETERS. Not if you look sharply at the average baby.
ROSE. *(Hand on her belly.)* How can you say that?
PETERS. If a baby had the strength, wouldn't he knock you down to get to a tit? Has a baby a conscience? If he could tear buildings apart to get to a suck, what would stop him? We tolerate babies only because they are helpless, but the alpha and omega of their real nature is a five-letter word, g-r-e-e-d. The rest is gossip. *(Calvin enters with Charlotte, both studying papers of figures. She sits down absorbed in papers, and working pocket calculator.)*

CALVIN. *(Absorbed in his figures.)* Harry.
PETERS. Yes? *(Calvin still doesn't look up.)* ... Did you call me Harry?
CALVIN. *(Surprised at himself.)* What?
PETERS. Charley ... come on ... *(Calvin stares at him as he approaches.)* It's me! *(Calvin stares front.)* Mother and Dad ... remember Mother and Dad? Fishing in Sheepshead Bay? The fluke? ... I know! — the bluefish, when you gutted that big bluefish and brought it over to ... what was her name! — Marcia ... yes, Marcia Levine!
CALVIN. Marcia Levine?
PETERS. In that shingle house on the corner! You said she had ... *(To the others.)* — excuse me, please — *(To Calvin.)* ... the best ass on the East Coast.
CALVIN. *(Very doubtfully, striving to recall.)* Marcia *Levine?*
PETERS. For God's sake, Calvin, you'd be in there whole *days* with her! *(Frantically — to all.)* Am I the only one who remembers anything? I'm going to fall off the earth! *(Furiously to Calvin.)* For God's sake, man, you'd lie on your bed looking up at the ceiling endlessly repeating, like a prayer, "Marcia Levine's ass, Marcia Levine's ass ... Marcia Levine has the most beautiful ass in America!"
CALVIN. I don't remember her ...
PETERS. *(Laughing happily.)* You have to step out of this ... this forgetfulness, Calvin! It's a terrible, terrible thing to forget Marcia Levine! ... Listen, you do know I'm Harry, don't you?
CALVIN. *(A remoteness coming over him.)* You're mistaking me for somebody else.
PETERS. No! Charley, I will not accept that! Charley? Please ... if you forget me ... don't you see? If you forget me — who ... *(With a desperate cry.)* who the hell am I! Charley, save me! *(Calvin is staring front, eyes dead. Peters roars in terror into his face.)* Man ... wake up your dead eyes! *(Calvin doesn't move. A moment.)* ... Sorry for troubling you. *(Closes his eyes in pain; slumps down on a seat. Pause.)* God, if no one remembers what I remember ... if no one remembers what I ... *(Cathy-May enters. She is in a tight white miniskirt, transparent blouse, carries a white purse and a brown shopping bag ... and wears a dog collar.)*

Why are you wearing a dog collar?

CATHY-MAY. Case I get lost, he said.

PETERS. Dear ... listen ... could I ask you...?

CATHY-MAY. Don't ask me too much, I might not be here by the end.

PETERS. Could I just listen to you?

CATHY-MAY. But don't take too long. And please don't hurt me. *(He presses his ear to her breast. She breathes in deeply, and exhales.)* You were loved, Harry. But I'm very tired.

PETERS. Please; more ... *(She inhales again.)* Yes! More! *(She does it again.)* Oh, glorious ... to hear a woman's deep breathing again! *(She breathes in and out again and again, her breaths coming faster and faster ... and now he is breathing with her.)* Oh Cathy-May, Cathy-May, Cathy-May...! *(Larry enters, walks over to her and rips the shopping bag out of her hand, turns it over — it is empty.)*

LARRY. This is shopping? Where's the stuff, left it on the counter again? *(Feels her for panties.)* And where's your underwear? *(To Peters.)* And this woman votes! Walks around bare-ass on New York streets? Bends over in the fruit market to test tomatoes in front of *Koreans?* — a married woman? What am I a fuckin' ox, I don't have feelings? Take her to a counselor and I'm behind her on the stairs and she's wearing no panties! — for a conference with a *counselor?* Meantime I'm overdue for a heart operation, so I'm not supposed to be stressed! Can you believe a fucking doctor telling me not to be stressed in the city of New York? And that idiot is going to operate on me! — Look at this! *(Shaking the bag.)* Look at this! ... Where's your underwear? You belong to me or not? I said you belong to me or not! Where is your underwear, stupid!! *(With a sweeping gesture he sends her onto her back, legs in the air, and looks under her skirt; she is struggling ineffectually to free herself.)* You see underwear, Mister? Look, everybody! *(He is trying to spread her legs apart.)* Forget your shoes and take a look at this! How can this belong to anybody! — Look at it!

CATHY-MAY. You were loved, Harry!

LARRY. *(Struggling with her legs.)* Show them, show them! Look at this, Professor! *(Peters, crying out, tries to intervene but the horror of it sends him away, rushing about, covering his eyes and yelling.)*

PETERS. Nonononono!
LARRY. *(To Peters.)* What are you scared of, come here and open your eyes! *(The struggle stops; Larry is kneeling beside Cathy-May now, kissing her gently. She has become inert. Peters comes and bends and presses his ear to her breast.)*
LEONARD. What do you hear?
PETERS. Footsteps. And darkness. Oh, how terrible to go into that darkness alone, alone! *(Cathy-May emits one last exhale ... Peters kisses his finger and touches it to her mouth.)*
CATHY-MAY. C-aaaaaaahh! *(And then she is still.)*
ADELE. I was a substitute teacher for six years in Weehauken, New Jersey. But little by little I came to realize that I am a brokenhearted person. That's all there was to it — I'm brokenhearted. Always was and would always be. At the same time I am often full of hope ... that for no particular reason I will wake up one morning and find that my sorrow has left me, just walked away, quiet as a pussycat in the middle of the night. I know it can happen ... *(She picks up her mirror and examines her face.)* I know it. I know it.
PETERS. *(Slight pause.)* — Rest now. All rest. Quietly, please. Quietly rest. While we think of the subject. While breath still comes blessedly clear. While we learn to be brave. *(Rose and Leonard sit on either side of Peters. Further U., frozen in time, Larry is looking into the empty shopping bag, Charlotte is working her calculator, Calvin is staring into space, Adele is examining her face in her mirror, turning from side to side. Light begins to die on these. Rose opens her eyes. Light dies on Leonard now, and only Rose and Peters are illuminated.)*
ROSE. Papa?
PETERS. *(Opens his eyes, listens.)* Yes?
ROSE. Please stay.
PETERS. *(Straight ahead.)* I'm trying!
ROSE. I love you, Papa.
PETERS. I'm trying as hard as I can. I love you, darling. I wonder ... could that be the subject! *(For a moment he is alone in light. It snaps out.)*

END

NEW PLAYS

- **TAKING SIDES by Ronald Harwood.** Based on the true story of one of the world's greatest conductors whose wartime decision to remain in Germany brought him under the scrutiny of a U.S. Army determined to prove him a Nazi. *"A brave, wise and deeply moving play delineating the confrontation between culture, and power, between art and politics, between irresponsible freedom and responsible compromise." --London Sunday Times.* [4M, 3W] ISBN: 0-8222-1566-7

- **MISSING/KISSING by John Patrick Shanley.** Two biting short comedies, MISSING MARISA and KISSING CHRISTINE, by one of America's foremost dramatists and the Academy Award winning author of *Moonstruck*. *"... Shanley has an unusual talent for situations ... and a sure gift for a kind of inner dialogue in which people talk their hearts as well as their minds...." --N.Y. Post.* MISSING MARISA [2M], KISSING CHRISTINE [1M, 2W] ISBN: 0-8222-1590-X

- **THE SISTERS ROSENSWEIG by Wendy Wasserstein, Pulitzer Prize-winning author of *The Heidi Chronicles*.** Winner of the 1993 Outer Critics Circle Award for Best Broadway Play. A captivating portrait of three disparate sisters reuniting after a lengthy separation on the eldest's 50th birthday. *"The laughter is all but continuous." --New Yorker. "Funny. Observant. A play with wit as well as acumen.... In dealing with social and cultural paradoxes, Ms. Wasserstein is, as always, the most astute of commentators." --N.Y. Times.* [4M, 4W] ISBN: 0-8222-1348-6

- **MASTER CLASS by Terrence McNally. Winner of the 1996 Tony Award for Best Play.** Only a year after winning the Tony Award for *Love! Valour! Compassion!*, Terrence McNally scores again with the most celebrated play of the year, an unforgettable portrait of Maria Callas, our century's greatest opera diva. *"One of the white-hot moments of contemporary theatre. A total triumph." --N.Y. Post. "Blazingly theatrical." -- USA Today.* [3M, 3W] ISBN: 0-8222-1521-7

- **DEALER'S CHOICE by Patrick Marber.** A weekly poker game pits a son addicted to gambling against his own father, who also has a problem but won't admit it. *"... make tracks to DEALER'S CHOICE, Patrick Marber's wonderfully masculine, razor-sharp dissection of poker-as-life.... It's a play that comes out swinging and never lets up -- a witty, wisecracking drama that relentlessly probes the tortured souls of its six very distinctive ... characters. CHOICE is a cutthroat pleasure that you won't want to miss." --Time Out (New York).* [6M] ISBN: 0-8222-1616-7

- **RIFF RAFF by Laurence Fishburne.** RIFF RAFF marks the playwriting debut of one of Hollywood's most exciting and versatile actors. *"Mr. Fishburne is surprisingly and effectively understated, with scalding bubbles of anxiety breaking through the surface of a numbed calm." --N.Y. Times. "Fishburne has a talent and a quality...[he] possesses one of the vital requirements of a playwright -- a good ear for the things people say and the way they say them." --N.Y. Post.* [3M] ISBN: 0-8222-1545-4

DRAMATISTS PLAY SERVICE, INC.
440 Park Avenue South, New York, NY 10016 212-683-8960 Fax 212-213-1539
postmaster@dramatists.com www.dramatists.com